Stop Smoking

A Concise Guide…

Author: John Pullen

Copyright © 2013 John Pullen

Publisher: John Pullen

First EBook Edition: 2013

This Edition: 2014

Printed by CreateSpace, An Amazon.com Company

Cover Image Design: Tom Clare

Available from Amazon.com, CreateSpace.com and other retail outlets

www.johnpullenwriter.com

To

Bernice and Jerry

Contents

"One thousand Americans

stop smoking every day

-by dying."

...Author Unknown

Introduction

Congratulations – give yourself a pat on the back. You have already overcome one of the most difficult barriers to giving up smoking forever. You have broken your cycle of inertia and done something about it. No more are you prepared to procrastinate about giving up. You have taken the first step and as on any journey, the first step is the most important. Without it you cannot move forwards. You are on your way to start a new chapter in your life; one filled with more health, wellbeing and happiness.

This book in the series can really help you to quit smoking and open up an opportunity to enjoy your life feeling healthier, fitter and happier about yourself.

If, at this stage, you feel you would like more information about the whole subject of Hypnotherapy and how it can help with many conditions and symptoms then try "Hypnotherapy" by the same author. It is also part of this series and available on Amazon and CreateSpace as well as other leading outlets.

The first part of this book details why some people smoke, the factors that keep them smoking even when they really want to quit and the issues involved in their decision whether to take the second step of stopping forever.

The next part describes your method of quitting – hypnotherapy. In plain words it explains how the method works and the ways you can use it to help you.

Finally, there is the Therapy Script which is your guide to a new healthier smoke free future. You have the choice whether to use the gist of the script (you don't need to memorise it) and use a technique called self-hypnosis or whether to record it yourself (or use a friend) and listen to it on an audio device. On the other hand, you may decide to use a registered hypnotherapist and there is some useful information on how to go about finding one.

There are also many people who may start to read the book, decide they are ready to quit and by the time they have finished it, they find that they have "automatically" become non-smokers. There is no one right answer but there are many to choose from.

Understanding a problem is usually the key to finding a solution…so let's start now.

"Giving up smoking is the easiest thing in the world.

I know because I've done it thousands of times."

...Mark Twain

Part 1

Can I Quit Smoking?

Willpower

You may be sitting or standing, either at home or in the workplace and be asking yourself this very question, "Can I quit smoking?" You may have friends or relatives who have given up almost as it may seem, on a whim. No planning, no hardship and no negative side effects. Lucky them.

On the other hand you almost certainly have a longer list of acquaintances who have tried numerous times to give up. Many of these will have succeeded using one of a variety of methods, willpower, patches, gums and hypnosis amongst others. It is also likely that some "failed." Perhaps they quit for a period of time and then for some reason or other, went back to smoking.

You probably know people who fit into each of these categories. As human beings we are a diverse bunch with different needs and desires. The reasons behind "success" or "failure" can be just as diverse. But if people were asked to name one attribute they think will be needed to bring about success in becoming a non-smoker, most would probably put "willpower" near the top of the list.

Wrong!

You do not need willpower to give up smoking. There will be a few individuals who will use sheer willpower to stop smoking and never go back to it. But these people will be in the minority. The rest of the would-be non-smokers need a little more help and a plan of action.

Point to Note

You don't need willpower to stop smoking

Using willpower alone is a conscious act and as we will see later on, the secret to long-lasting success lies in the unconscious mind. It is all about re-programming your mind not to need cigarettes in the future; in fact not to need them in your life at all.

Exercise

The Self-Image Reprogrammer

As an initial exercise to help set you up for your new life as a non-smoker, take a couple of minutes out to do the following.

As with all exercises and especially with the Therapy Script, do not listen to or attempt any of the exercises unless it is safe for you to do so. That means you do not listen to or practice them if you are driving or using any machinery.

Close your eyes and relax. Now imagine you are looking at another you in the not too distant future. As you look closer, you realise that it is you as a non-smoker. Notice how you seem to stand more upright, looking more confident, relaxed and happy. Spend a few moments enjoying seeing the new non-smoking you.

Now, in your mind's eye, step into the new you. Immerse yourself and become one person. See through the eyes of the new you. Hear through their ears. Most of all, feel what it is like to be a non-smoker. Breathe deeply and feel the oxygen entering your lungs. Allow the positive energy of feeling fitter and healthier permeate every cell of your mind and body.

Feels good doesn't it?

Enjoy these new feelings for a minute or two and when you are ready simply say to yourself, "I am going to count up to three and when I reach three, I will open my eyes and feel really refreshed and ready to go forwards to a smoke-free future."

So ready, "1...2...3. Open your eyes. Feel really good about yourself and excited for the future."

You can practice any of the exercises in this book whenever you wish as long as it is safe and appropriate to do so. The more you practice them the more they will become a part of the new you and the positive feelings associated with them will also become second nature to you.

Point to Note

Practice the exercises and the new positive feelings will become a part of you.

They will become hard-wired into your unconscious mind.

So, if you don't need willpower, what do you need to bring to the therapy session?

Motivation

To some, these two terms (willpower and motivation) may seem quite similar but they are not. In this context, motivation can be looked on as how high your desire is to give up smoking. Willpower is a measure of the conscious effort you put into giving up. But as we will discuss later on, hypnotherapy is all about working with the unconscious mind. So once again, you don't need willpower to be successful at quitting smoking.

We now need to look a little deeper into what we mean by motivation. It is all very well saying that you want to give up smoking but do you really mean the words that have just been written; that "**you**" want to give up smoking.

It is not unusual for potential clients to ring up my practice and ask if I can help them to give up smoking. I would normally enquire "why do you want to quit?" and quite often the reply is along the lines of "my husband/wife wants me to" or "so and so sent me."

These responses are not assertive; they may indicate that the person is feeling pressurised into giving up but deep down their heart is not in it. Unless you personally really want to give up, then any treatment may not be as effective as it could be.

Point to Note

You must want to quit for yourself, not for someone else.

There are a number of factors which can come into play and affect the motivation of the subject. Perhaps the number one motivator is when the client rings up and says, "I've just come from my doctor and I've got...." This doesn't usually mean cancer but they may have other conditions linked to smoking and are a severe warning sign of what might happen to them in the future unless they take action now. Believe me they really know what motivation is. But waiting for that "scare" is a very, very bad idea.

Point to Note

Do not wait for the doctor to say have a disease.

There are far more healthier and positive reasons to consider when deciding whether to quit. If you have children, are you setting them a good example? Will taking a chance of dying before your time be fair on them and the rest of your family? Are you in any way exposing them to second-hand smoke; it is easier to do than many people think.

From a personal point of view, have you noticed whether you are getting "puffed out" when running for a bus or walking up the stairs? Do you generally feel unfit? Have you or more likely, other people around you noticed the stale smell of tobacco on your clothing and breath? Do you in any way feel apart when you excuse yourself from the office or from company in order to go outside to light up?

These are all good reasons for you as an individual to consider carefully. So be honest and ask yourself the following question.

Do I really want to give up smoking for my own personal reasons?

If your honest answer is "Yes" then you have a very good chance of becoming a non-smoker and then to remain as a non-smoker.

"(Smoking) It helps fight boredom.

It gives you more to do and less time to do it in."

...Moshin Hamid

Part 2

Why We Smoke

The Body Under Attack

There are many reasons why we start to smoke and even more why we continue the habit. But before we look at some of the common triggers that keep us smoking, let's first consider what smoking does to your body when you start and what happens to it when you persist over a longer period of time.

Let's not beat around the bush here; smoking is a poison to your system. It introduces toxins into your body which have a dramatic effect on your own body and brain chemistry. Many people are aware of the chemical nicotine which is present in tobacco smoke and most are also aware that it is the part that is responsible for the "addiction."

Point to Note

Smoking poisons your body – FACT.

When you inhale the smoke, nicotine has the effect of "stressing" your body. This results in your body trying to protect itself and it does this by releasing chemicals of its own such as endorphins and endomorphines. Their purpose is to act as natural painkillers and to fight off the effects felt by the toxins.

Our minds and bodies are amazing; there are many, many means we have at our disposal to ward off attacks from outside factors. And they all come to our aid without us consciously asking for their help.

However, these "good" chemicals are limited. So our body stops the natural release of them and instead decides to keep them back in case of any future attacks from this "smoke enemy." Now the usual effect of these "good" chemicals is to make us feel relaxed and happier. So if they are now being held back, we begin to feel stress and our body starts to miss these "feel good" natural supplements.

From the point of view of the smoker, they are experiencing feelings of anxiety and tension. So what do they deduce from this? Their "logical" reasoning is to believe that they are suffering from the symptoms of stress or something similar and the only way to relieve these symptoms is to have another cigarette.

Of course, when they do have that next cigarette the body releases the held-back endorphins in order to fight back against the invasion of smoke. The result; the smoker feels a bit better and immediately attributes this to the cigarette alone. However, the truth of the matter is that the real culprit is the cigarette.

Point to Note

Tobacco intake can be the cause of stress symptoms, not the cure.

The next exercise is a very effective one you can practice which will help to really put you off wanting to smoke or have a cigarette near your mouth. It isn't pleasant, but it works.

Exercise

Repugnance by Association

Much of hypnotherapy is taken up using positive suggestions and exercises to help us to move forwards to a new healthier and fitter lifestyle. And these techniques are extremely effective for many conditions. However, there is also a part of therapy which concentrates on associating something that the patient dislikes intensely and associating it with the habit of smoking a cigarette.

Close your eyes and relax. Concentrate gently on your breathing until you feel your body relaxing and your mind feeling focused. Now, imagine something that really disgusts you. And by that I mean something that can make you feel sick just by the smell of it. If the sight and prospect of tasting it makes you want to throw up then all the better.

Don't feel limited in your choice. Over the years I have heard all sorts of things which disgust people, so let your imagination run wild. When you have selected one that is particularly repugnant to you, imagine the smell of it. Now, press the thumb and forefinger of your left hand together. This is called an Anchor and its function is to form an association with the smell and the pressing together of the thumb and forefinger of your left hand.

Later on you will be able to use an exercise called The Anchor which will use the thumb and forefinger of your right hand to induce positive feelings of calmness. So it is important not to get the two mixed up!

Okay, you are pressing together the thumb and forefinger of your left hand and thinking of that really horrible smell. Now I want you to also see that object of revulsion in your mind's eye and keep pressing your finger and thumb together. It should increase your feelings of nausea.

Now begin to bring that object closer to your mouth. The smell will intensify and the sight will sicken you even more. Put the object in your mouth and keep pressing. At this point you will probably feeling ready to be sick. Stop if you think you are going to be but start the exercise again after a few moments.

The idea is that you should practice this exercise until the pressing together of the thumb and forefinger of your left hand sufficiently produces these horrible feelings each time. When you have achieved this you are ready for the final part of this exercise.

Press them together again and feel all those feelings of sickness and revulsion. Now, imagine bringing a cigarette closer to your mouth. The smell of the cigarette is overpowered by the smell of that object. The sight of the cigarette is overshadowed by the image of the object. Finally, as you try to put the cigarette in your mouth, you will imagine that revolting object is being put in your mouth instead and all you can taste is that object.

I never said it would be pleasant but if you are prepared to practice this exercise, you may find that your desire to smoke has gone away. For many, this is enough to put them off smoking for good. But for the rest of us, we still have many more weapons in our arsenal.

Now let's take a look at some of the reasons why we smoke and with the reason why so many people start to smoke in the first place.

Peer Pressure

As part of the usual Case History I always take when I first meet a client, one of the questions I ask a smoker who wishes to quit is, "When did you start and why?"

By far the most common answer is, "I started between 14 and 16 years of age and I began because some of my friends smoked and I didn't want to feel left out." This is simple peer pressure at a time in their lives where they are looking to fit in and be accepted by their circle of friends.

Point to Note

Many start in their teens in order to fit in with their friends.

When questioned further, their first experiences with tobacco were not very pleasant. It is common to hear reports of feeling sick, bouts of dizziness and having headaches. Why might this be? It's because their body is fighting to repel the smoke and associated poisons entering them.

Your body never liked you smoking. It never did and it never will. All that happens over time is that your body has to adjust to the fact that you now smoke. But it is always ready for you to stop and it can then return to "normal" service.

You can forgive yourself for allowing "peer pressure" to initiate your smoking habit. However, as an adult who knows the truth about smoking and the very real dangers to your health, it is really a "no brainer" when it comes to considering whether to give up or not.

Stress

As we saw earlier, the stress state causes certain chemicals to be produced in the mind and body. This stress response goes right back to the beginning of human existence. Many people will have heard of the "fight or flight" reflex. Basically what this says is that if we are confronted by a threat, our body immediately prepares itself for a choice in the course of action it wishes to take.

Let's take the classic example. One of our ancient ancestors is out hunting wild game for the next meal and he comes across a wild animal which is bigger and meaner than he was expecting. Suddenly his weapons are no guarantee to success. He has to make a choice; to stay and fight or run away as fast as he can. There is a third choice; he could freeze but we will concentrate on the first two.

Whichever choice he makes, he will still require to be ready to execute his action. This means that his mind and body must be prepared. And it is. Thanks to this reflex, at the first sign of danger blood was diverted from systems which were no longer important such as the stomach and pumped into the legs and arms. These limbs will be needed no matter what choice is made.

The chemicals now washing through his body include adrenalin and cortisol. They will help him to fight or run away. When the danger is past, assuming he has not become lunch, the chemicals that helped him are no longer needed. So in a normal state of affairs, they are replaced with new chemicals which help to relax the mind and body and restore it to its original state.

The problem arises if the person remains aroused and ready to fight or run even if there is no threat. The mind and body remain in a state of readiness with the wrong sort of chemicals washing around. If nothing is done to relieve the situation the person concerned becomes stressed and anxious and will most likely develop symptoms associated with somebody suffering from a stress disorder.

Now it is also true to say that some stress in our lives now and again is good for us. If we didn't experience some stress, we wouldn't move forward in our lives. So some stress is good but we must not let it get out of hand. If we do, then we will often try to find a way to relieve it. And that is where smoking comes back into the picture.

Many people suffering from stress choose the wrong methods in order to try and control it. Smoking, as we saw in the previous section is one of them. Excessive alcohol consumption is another along with the use of leisure drugs. All of these will compound the problem and make things worse.

We already know that the cigarette which the smoker feels is relieving the stress temporarily is actually causing the stress to become worse and in the future they will require more tobacco. And so the circle tightens.

Instead, it is much more sensible to use other direct methods to relieve your stress. And there are many to choose from. One of the most common is called "The Anchor" and is used by many hypnotherapists to help a patient find relaxation. Just follow the instructions and if you practice often, it will soon become hard-wired into your mind and the effects more powerful. But remember, as with all these Exercises, only use them when it is safe and appropriate to do so. Read through the exercise before attempting it for yourself.

Exercise

The Anchor

First sit down comfortably and relax for a few moments. Now, allow your mind to drift to a place, it can be real or imaginary, where you feel totally relaxed, safe and happy. It can be a holiday destination, your home or anywhere.

Allow your thoughts of this place to become sharper in your mind. Begin to see details around this place. Hear the sounds you would expect to hear and any smells. If it is a sunny day, then feel the warmth of the sun. Bring as many of your senses into play as you can.

Then, when you are ready and really enjoying your special place of relaxation, I want you to press the thumb and forefinger of your right hand together. And when you do, increase all of the pleasant sensations you are experiencing. Hold your thumb and forefinger together for about ten seconds and in that time try to increase the good sensations you are feeling.

Next release your finger and thumb and relax for a few moments before repeating the exercise. Do this a few times and try to practice it often. You will soon find that as your thumb and forefinger press together, the good feelings will flood in and you will automatically relax and feel a lot better.

You can use this technique whenever you are under pressure or feel stressed. Just remember to make sure it is safe for you to do so.

Boredom

Boredom can be the trigger to a number of bad coping strategies. Not only can it be responsible for lighting up that next cigarette, it can also be the reason why some people start to drink too much and carry out their drinking alone which is a dangerous sign.

In the last section we saw how stress can wrongly lead smokers to have a cigarette believing that it is a cure to feeling the symptoms of stress. Likewise the feelings associated with being lonely and bored can lead to using smoking as a way for you to have something to do with your hands and mouth. Remember also that you do not have to be alone to feel lonely and bored.

Many can find themselves isolated in an uncaring relationship. Some people feel that their jobs are so mundane that they happily take a "cigarette break" just to break the monotony of the work. Boredom is a state which comes about due to a lack of stimulation. And to be blunt, whether you find stimulation in your life or not is a personal choice.

I know that if you are feeling lonely and your mood is low, then it can be difficult to break the cycle. But you should consider trying to break this cycle. However, it is important here to say that if you really are feeling low or depressed, you should go and see your doctor for some professional help. Depression can creep up on you.

But for the rest of us, it is important to recognise if boredom is a factor in your smoking habit. If it is then try to stimulate yourself by going out and taking a class or joining a group. Not all of these charge money to join. The message here is that it is all very well successfully giving up smoking but it is also important to be aware of what your triggers are and then to try to minimise them.

The Therapy Script does address these points but it is helpful to understand where your urges to smoke come from as well.

Low Mood

This is something we touched on in the last section. It can be tied up with a number of conditions and circumstances. Low mood can cause a person to need something to "pick them up" or just make them feel better for a short time.

Eating fatty foods is one example of a bad coping strategy. A large bar of chocolate will give someone a "sugar rush" and make them feel better for a short time. However, when it wears off, quite often the original feelings of low mood are joined by new feelings of guilt at having eaten the bar in the first place. This compounds the problem and doesn't help anyone.

And of course smoking is another bad way of dealing with low mood. We already know that the temporary "high" smokers get from their inhalation of tobacco makes them feel a little better but we also know that the act of smoking is going to lead to their next "low". In fact it is the cause of it and leads to that tightening of the circle.

One of the many ways of coping with low mood is exercise. And that doesn't mean you have to immediately go out and start training for the next marathon. In fact, if you are unfit or badly overweight, it is a good idea to see your doctor and get some advice before you start exercising.

However, exercise does not have to involve Olympic style training regimes; walking a little quicker than normal is a good way to start. Get off the bus one stop earlier and walk the rest of the way. Climb the stairs at work rather than get the lift or just get out a floor early and walk. There are many gentle and safe ways to start.

Why do I recommend exercise? Because even gentle exercise releases the right sort of natural chemicals into the mind and body and they help to give you that same "high" but in a more natural and healthy way. Try it and your body and mind will thank you for it.

Addiction

Every smoker probably knows smoking can quite easily escalate into an addiction; a physical and mental need to maintain the intake of tobacco smoke into the body. And most also are aware that the ingredient responsible for the addictive element of tobacco is nicotine.

Make no mistake, nicotine has strong addictive qualities. But I would like to ask you a question. How long do you think nicotine stays in your body after you give up smoking? The answer may surprise you. It is usually between 24 and 36 hours. That's all. Okay, you may still experience cravings after that but it is important to bear this time period in mind.

Point to Note

Nicotine only stays in the body for between 24 & 36 hours.

It is one of the reasons why hypnotherapists tell their patients not to use nicotine patches or gums if they choose hypnotherapy to become a non-smoker. With the correct treatment, you don't need them.

I am certainly not saying that they are no good; in fact their use is one of the recommended ways of quitting smoking. But hypnotherapy is different; it uses a different approach which does not require you to drip-feed nicotine into your system. In fact there have been some reported cases of smokers becoming addicted to the patches after they gave up smoking.

When considering quitting smoking you should not overstate the addictive qualities of tobacco. They can be addressed using hypnotherapy.

Habit

Smoking is most certainly a habit and a habit is defined as a routine or behaviour that is repeated regularly and tends to occur on a subconscious level.

All it usually requires are for one or more factors to be present in a particular situation and they trigger a reaction from the person concerned. And in this case, the reaction is another cigarette being lit up.

These triggers can be emotional or environmental. We've already discussed some of the emotional triggers that smokers may react to. The environmental triggers are places or situations. For example, in the days when people were allowed to smoke in pubs and bars, it would not be unusual to be told by a smoker that once they had a drink in their hand, they suddenly found that it was joined by a lit cigarette.

The other interesting point was that most said they were not really consciously aware of deciding to have a cigarette; it was an unconscious decision and action. Their reaction to having a drink was to have a cigarette; it was a habit which had become hard-wired into their mind. After all, what does the proverb say? Practice makes perfect.

This is another reason why hypnotherapy can be so effective in stopping smoking because it works with the unconscious and lays down new neural pathways which lead to the smoker substituting more healthy reactions to these triggers. It is always a good idea to work out what your triggers are before undergoing therapy.

This usually takes the form of a "Smoking Diary" and this is what we shall look at in the next section.

Environmental Triggers

In the previous section, we considered one example of an environmental trigger; the drink in a pub. There are many others and I would like you to spend a few minutes writing out a list of triggers which affect you personally; places and situations where you "automatically" reach for the packet of cigarettes.

To help you with some ideas which are common to many and to illustrate how you might construct your diary, there is an example on the right.

Smoking Diary

0700: Get out of bed, make a cup of tea and have a cigarette.

0730: Finish breakfast and have a cigarette.

0800: Waiting for bus and have a cigarette.

0845: Walking to office and have cigarette.

1030: Cigarette break.

1230: After lunch and two cigarettes.

1500: Cigarette break.

1730: Walk to bus stop and have a cigarette.

1815: Get home, put kettle on and have a cigarette.

1900: Preparing dinner and have a cigarette.

2000: Relax in front of the TV and have three cigarettes.

2300: Last cigarette before going to bed.

This is a list which may cover some of the smoking triggers many people encounter in their day to day life. Yours will probably be different but I'm sure you will recognise some of the triggers mentioned.

Remember also that the above diary is for a weekday for somebody who works away from home. It is advisable to construct a diary covering your weekend smoking as well.

Point to Note

Make a separate list out for weekends

At the end, count up the number of cigarettes you smoke in a week. You may or may not be surprised. In the example above the daily intake is 15. More of the cost and health implications will be discussed in a later section.

"Trying to quit smoking…

The best way to quit is to simply not buy them.

"I can't" generally means "I choose not to."

…Stanley Victor Paskavich

Part 3

Ready to Quit – Yes or No?

At this point you should be in a positive state of mind and ready to quit smoking forever and become a non-smoker. But just in case you are still procrastinating, here are a few practical reasons why it is a good idea to kick the habit once and for all. Let's start with some of the negative issues associated with being a smoker.

Negative Issues

As with the Positive Issues later, we will split them into two groups; Health and Financial issues.

Health and Illness

No one should still be under the illusion that smoking is good for you. It is not and there is plenty of medical evidence to prove it. I know that some smokers will come back with the retort that they know someone who has smoked 40 a day for the last 30 years and is still in good health.

Well, lucky them. It still doesn't take away from the majority of smokers who with the same track record may be exhibiting a whole range of different medical problems including a number of types of cancer. You may look at the "healthy" smoker in the example above and say they are the exception that proves the rule.

But if there are a couple of smokers out there who still doubt the medical evidence, here are some figures for the UK which may change your mind. Being statistics they apply to the general population but I think the message is loud and clear.

Each cigarette shortens your life by 5.5 minutes.

That's nearly 2 hours for every packet of 20 cigarettes.

Smoking causes 4 times as many deaths as road, suicide and drug deaths put together.

70% of lung cancer deaths are caused by cigarette smoking.

25% of heart disease deaths are caused by smoking.

90% of emphysema deaths and bronchial diseases are caused by smoking.

Spend a few moments seriously considering these figures and then ask yourself whether you really want to take the chance of dying before your time.

Financial Worries

Even if some smokers may disagree over the medical evidence on smoking, one thing that most smokers will agree on is the ever rising price of a packet of cigarettes. Unless you are quite well off the cost of smoking 20 a day really adds up over a year. If you've never bothered to work it out or haven't taken in the price rises over the last few years, here's a bit of a shock for you.

Assume you smoke about 20 cigarettes each day.

That's 365 days (we'll let you off leap years).

Let's also take the average price of a packet of 20 as £6-50.

This is approximately correct for late 2012.

Therefore the cost of smoking per year is <u>£2,372-50</u>.

That's a lot of money to burn in anyone's book.

Positive Issues

Let's now look at the same two criteria from the point of view of a person becoming a non-smoker.

Health and Fitness

Perhaps the most effective way of showing a smoker how their health and fitness improves when they quit is by listing the changes their body undergoes after they stop. Some of the changes are very rapid, whilst others naturally take a bit longer. But the one thing they all have in common is that they all contribute to you enjoying a healthier and hopefully much longer life.

When you stop smoking, within;-

20 minutes your blood pressure and heart rate return to normal for that individual.

Hand and foot temperatures return to normal. This is because nicotine constricts blood flow in the veins.

8 hours carbon monoxide levels decrease back into the normal range.

Oxygen levels increase into the normal range.

24 - 36 hours nicotine is finally eliminated from your body.

Your senses of taste and smell return.

72 hours lung capacity starts to increase as the tar from tobacco begins to leave the body.

During this period you may experience symptoms similar to having a cold but these will stop soon after.

1 – 9 months coughing decreases and energy levels increase. Most non-smokers I have treated notice these changes beginning after only a couple of weeks.

5 years your chances of dying from lung cancer are significantly reduced.

Becoming a non-smoker means that you start to enjoy some of the health benefits almost straight away and can likely look forward to feeling fitter and healthier for years to come.

More Spending Power

We saw that smoking a packet of 20 a day can easily cost over £2,000 per year. That's a lot of money and I also strongly believe that when you become a non-smoker, you should be rewarded.

Therefore, I always recommend to my clients that they open another bank account and put the money they are saving on cigarettes into it and then treat themselves. You shouldn't feel you must spend it on essentials; after all, you were just letting it go up in smoke before. So do what I suggest and think what you might spend it on.

From the feedback I have received in the past, a number of people take the getting fitter part of being a non-smoker further by joining a gym. Others go on expensive holidays. And some just hit the shops. It doesn't matter what you spend it on as long as you view it as a treat; as your just reward for becoming a non-smoker.

"There is no such thing as "just one last cigarette" –

except the last cigarette that you've already had."

...H.M. Forester

Part 4

Make the Change Now

Well you've got this far and you've read the pros and cons. In the case of smoking I've not found a pro in favour of continuing, so it's all go to becoming a non-smoker. All it needs is for you to commit. If you are genuinely ready to quit smoking because YOU want to become a non-smoker, then answer the following question honestly to yourself.

Do YOU really want to become a non-smoker NOW?

If the answer is YES, then read on.

Exercise

The Positive Affirmation

This short exercise is to set you up ready to make these new positive changes to your life by becoming a non-smoker. Close your eyes and just gently focus on your breathing. Feel your body begin to relax and your mind becoming calmer.

Next I want you to think back to a time when you felt positive about yourself and self-confident. If you find this a bit difficult at first, then try to think of something that you achieved. It doesn't have to be anything really big, just something which you were proud of. By thinking of it now, you feel a little glow or warmth from the memory.

Spend a few moments getting used to that memory and the positive feelings from it. When you are ready I would like you to increase your positive experience by making the image bigger and brighter. If there are any sounds associated with your memories then make them louder. Continue to enhance all of these factors and experience your feelings getting stronger and more positive. Allow these feelings to travel and spread around your whole body. Let your self-confidence grow within you.

Now think about the challenge ahead of you. You are going to become a non-smoker because that is your decision and nothing is going to stop you from achieving your goal. Say to yourself, "I am a Non-Smoker. I don't smoke."

Say it loud and clear in your mind – "I am a Non-Smoker. I don't smoke."

Repeat it a few times and then relax with a feeling of pride and excitement, ready to meet your challenge and win.

"The believing we do something when we do nothing

is the first illusion of tobacco."

…Ralph Waldo Emerson

Part 5

Hypnotherapy – Your Way to Win

In this section we shall look at how hypnosis works in a clinical setting. We shall also banish some of the myths about hypnosis and try to answer some frequently asked questions. For a more detailed account of the theory and practice of hypnotherapy, you should read "Hypnotherapy" in this series. Available through Amazon and CreateSpace.

How it Works

To understand the basis of how hypnotherapy works, we should first discuss the mind and the central nervous system or CNS. The CNS as a whole consists of a number of parts with different functions. They are the brain, the spinal chord, peripheral nervous system and autonomic nervous system or ANS.

The brain is possibly the most sophisticated and complicated thing that has ever existed; at least as far as we know at present. It can be described as a number of control rooms because we now understand that different parts of the brain are responsible for different functions.

The spinal chord can be found within your spinal column and it connects the brain with the peripheral nervous system. Together they pass messages to and from the brain.

The final part is the autonomic nervous system. And what differentiates this part from the rest of the CNS is that it needs no conscious thought to activate it. In fact it can be looked upon as a type of auto-pilot, keeping many of our vital systems in check and functioning correctly. After all you don't have to tell yourself consciously to remember to breathe or to keep your temperature within strict limits. It happens automatically or unconsciously and is therefore a vital part of the whole system.

The important point to note in all this is that we can look at our mind and say there are two types of mind operating; a conscious mind and an unconscious mind. And this is very important in understanding how hypnosis works.

Now when a person experiences a hypnotic trance, they are usually feeling pleasantly relaxed. This activates the part of the ANS we call the para-sympathetic nervous system and it takes over from the "awake and active" sympathetic component.

The unconscious mind now becomes more prominent and there is a feature of it which allows hypnotherapy to be used effectively; namely the unconscious mind is open to direct suggestions. In the trance state, positive suggestions to help the patient adopt new healthier habits can be given. And because the unconscious does not analyse as the conscious mind does, these new healthier patterns of behaviour are accepted.

That is the basis on which hypnotherapy works. It is not magic but it is still pretty amazing.

Frequently Asked Questions

There are many myths and urban legends surrounding hypnosis. So let's now spend a few minutes setting the record straight.

How Old is the Study of Hypnosis?

Hypnosis in one form or another can be traced back thousands of years to Egyptian Dream Temples where a person would be put into a "sleep-like" state and then a physician of the temple would then "heal" the person with their powers.

Since then hypnosis has fallen into and out of favour. Mesmerism during the Victorian era was popular but was eventually proved to be based on very dubious science. Sigmund Freud was known to have practiced it before moving on and developing psychoanalysis.

During the First World War, hypnosis was successfully used in treating pain as well as "shell shock" now better understood as post-traumatic stress disorder. Unfortunately the condition was not understood until a number of soldiers had been court-martialled and shot for cowardice.

The years 1955 and 1958 mark important landmarks in the history of hypnosis. For it was in 1955 that the British Medical Association or BMA recommended that hypnosis should form part of a medical student's training. Then in 1958, France made similar recommendations in the training of their future doctors. Today, nurses associated to the Royal College of Nursing can take courses in clinical hypnosis.

Finally, we now come to the person that most hypnotherapists regard as the "father of modern hypnosis" Milton Erickson. The many and varied techniques he developed and pioneered are used by hypnotherapists the world over. His contributions have had a greater effect on the practice of hypnotherapy than anyone else.

Hypnotherapy now has its rightful place in the "talking therapies."

Is Hypnotherapy the same as Stage Hypnosis?

In a word, no. The main aim of stage hypnosis is entertainment. And from a number of quarters, even the term entertainment may be a bit dubious when used in this context.

With hypnotherapy, the client's needs come first. Every effort is made to make the whole session a positive and pleasurable experience.

Although there are very few conditions in which hypnotherapy is contra-indicated, there are some including schizophrenia and epilepsy. That is the reason why every registered hypnotherapist will take a full clinical and psychological case history before conducting the first therapy session. This is rarely carried out in the stage environment.

My own personal perspective on the subject is that with stage hypnosis the hypnotist takes the role of "master" over his subjects and "controls" the actions of those on stage. With hypnotherapy the client remains in control. And if you are about to ask how, then that is the next question I shall answer.

In Therapy, Who is in Control?

In the last answer I said the client and not the hypnotist is in charge. The reason is because although the client may be in a relaxed state of mind or trance, they are also aware of what is being said to them.

Therefore the client is in control and can always decline to accept any therapeutic suggestions made to them. That is why the therapist will always try to agree beforehand with the client what it is they want to achieve through hypnotherapy.

It is also the reason why you cannot be made to do anything you don't want to do. So films like "The Manchurian Candidate" can't turn you into an assassin who is going to try and kill the President of the United States (as shown in the movie). Unless you are already an assassin! (Joke, I hope).

Is Amnesia a Side-Effect?

No it isn't for the reasons given in the previous answer. It is possible that you may not totally remember every part of the therapy session but that is normal and no need for you to worry. You may feel as though you are drifting in and out of a trance-like state. This is both a normal and pleasant experience.

Will I Put on Weight?

This is a common question and concern for many people. The therapy session takes this into account and delivers suggestions that you will not substitute anything for the cigarettes you have left in the past.

If anything, many people have found their own self-control and self-discipline has been increased with the result that they feel more in control of other areas of their life as well. If there are any urges to feel the need to do something with your hands or mouth, suggestions such as sipping a cool, clear glass of water usually does the trick.

Self-Hypnosis

Self-hypnosis is a skill which can be easily learned with a little bit of practice. It can be said to be similar in some ways to meditation and yogic visualisations. All of the therapy options outlined except the hypnotherapist one involve self-hypnosis to some extent or another.

Perhaps the simplest way to approach the therapy stage of this guide is just to read through the therapy script. If you do decide on this method which requires the least effort on your part, then I would suggest that when you reach the script you make yourself comfortable and spend a few moments relaxing. Check that you will not be disturbed for about 30-40 minutes.

When you begin reading, don't force yourself to concentrate too much. Instead read at a comfortable and relaxed pace. Let the words sink in and allow yourself time to ponder their message to you. Imagine as though it is your unconscious mind that is reading to you. Both your unconscious and conscious mind will begin to take the positive suggestions to heart and they may begin to overwrite the old habits that you are about to leave in the past.

Oh and one obvious point; if you decide on this method, you do not have to close your eyes as reading can be a bit difficult if you do.

If you wish to pause, then do so. Perhaps allow your eyes to close whilst you think more deeply about what you are reading. Let the messages become personal to you. Your subconscious mind really does have the power to alter your old behaviours. Feel relaxed and positive as you continue. At the end of the script, relax for a few minutes with your eyes closed and ponder upon some of the final messages you have just read. The future for you can be smoke-free and you can live your life by being the person you really want to be.

Although it requires a bit more application and practice, if you decide to "learn" the gist of the therapy script, I suggest the best course of action is to practice it in stages and building up to the full script.

Begin with the eye closure and progressive relaxation. Get used to "letting go" and gradually add more stages until you feel comfortable with the whole script. Remember you do not have to be word perfect, but it does require you to build up your skill over time.

Audio Aids

A method of shortening the practice stages as outlined above is to record the therapy scripts onto an audio device.

You can do this by using your own voice or by asking a friend to record it for you. The tone of voice should reflect the content of the script. For example, the progressive relaxation part should be delivered using a quiet and relaxed tone of voice. By contrast the parts which suggest you to "Stop Smoking" should be in a much more authoritative tone.

It is worth persevering until you are happy with the result. Then just sit or lay back, make yourself comfortable and relax.

Hypnotherapy CDs

If all the above seems too hard, you can always purchase the full therapy sessions professionally recorded by the author and they can be found at;-

www.hypnohealthservices.com

There are many other such CDs on the market in both bookshops and online.

Using a Registered Hypnotherapist

If this guide has inspired you by understanding why people smoke and how it can be relatively simple to quit and you would like to use the most effective means to give up, then you should look to employing the services of a registered hypnotherapist.

There are many advertised in such listings as Yellow Pages, Thompsons' and on the Web. I would advise you to check out the qualifications and which professional body they are registered with.

Although there are a number of good organisations to choose from, I would personally recommend my own governing body, the British Society of Clinical Hypnosis. They can be found at;-

www.bsch.org.uk

"Cigarettes are killers that travel in packs."

…Author Unknown

Part 6

The Therapy Session Explained

The typical therapy session usually consists of six stages; each one perhaps overlapping but adding up to an effective way to bring positive results to the client. They are;-

Eye Closure

Progressive Relaxation

Deepening

Therapy

Ego-Boosting

Awakening

We will now look at each of these in turn, so that you will understand how they fit and work effectively together. Preparation is important and you should try to ensure that you are comfortable, in a quiet environment and you can reasonably expect not to be interrupted for the next 40 minutes or so.

If you are interrupted, don't worry; you will find that you will immediately be alert and can attend to whatever has occurred. You can always start again when things have quietened down.

However, if you are seeing a professional hypnotherapist, you can expect the first twenty minutes or so to be taken up with a detailed case history of yourself. Once again for more information about case histories, you should check "Hypnotherapy" also in this series.

Eye Closure

The first stage is known as eye closure and as its name implies, it is designed to encourage you to close your eyes and begin the relaxation stage. There are many ways to achieve this especially when the session is being conducted by a therapist.

But in the context of using self-hypnosis, it is most effective to first make yourself comfortable, either by sitting in a chair or lying down on a sofa or bed and just let your eyes close. Another tip is to first screw your eyes tightly shut. Wait a few seconds. Open them again and then let them close gently. The release of tension is very noticeable and closing your eyes feels really good.

Other methods suggest you concentrate your vision on a particular spot. After a while the eyes begin to feel tired and strained. You then feel the need to close them in order to release the tension. When you do, the release enables you to feel more relaxed and ready for the next stage.

Progressive Relaxation

This next stage focuses on relaxing your body and this is normally achieved in stages. Once again there are many ways to accomplish this.

The method used in the script is one where you imagine a warm wave of relaxation entering your body through your toes, slowly passing around your instep and heel and finally moving up to your ankles. As it does so, you may feel your feet become a little warmer and perhaps lighter.

However, there is no hard and fast rule to say you will experience these feelings. Your mind may interpret the suggestions in a different way and you could feel your feet becoming cooler and heavier. The important point is that it doesn't matter; your mind will work in its own way. But no matter how your mind interprets things, the one feeling you should notice is that your feet feel relaxed.

Remember relaxation is a learned experience. If you are currently feeling stressed, then feeling relaxed will not come naturally. You may have to practice this part. There is a bonus to this though. If you are feeling stressed out at any time, use the progressive relaxation part to help you to relax. It is a very effective treatment for stress in its own right.

The script moves on to suggest that the warm wave of relaxation passes up through your whole body and finishes in your mind. At the end of this stage you should be feeling physically relaxed in all your muscle groups and more calm and peaceful in your thoughts. This sets you up for the next stage; deepening.

Deepening

The deepening stage intends to do what it says; deepen your trance or state of relaxation. Once again there are many ways to achieve this and some schools of thought include the progressive relaxation into the deepening stage. I prefer to look on them as separate stages which lead into each other seamlessly.

In the case of our script I use a number of guided exercises and suggestions to help you to relax more and completely let go. It includes a countdown; with each number allowing you to go deeper. There are also trigger words which when mentioned suggest you just let go of any tension and accept your new relaxed state as being desirable.

At the conclusion of this stage you should be feeling relaxed in your body and calm in your mind. In this state you are ready and happy to accept the positive suggestions which will be delivered during the therapy stage of the session.

Therapy

This is the part responsible for making those changes in your life which you really want to make. In the case of Stopping Smoking there are a range of techniques and suggestions intended to achieve this.

The way they are delivered through the tone of voice can also be important here. A large part of the script is uplifting and encouraging. But there are other areas where the content is still positive but is authoritative in tone. For example, "You are a NON-SMOKER which means YOU NEVER SMOKE. YOU NEVER SMOKE AGAIN." You get the idea.

There is also a small part devoted to aversion therapy which has the effect of linking a cigarette with something you hate the smell and taste of. This example will be personal to you and can be anything you wish. Although it is not as pleasant as the rest of the session, it can be an important component to quitting for good.

Ego-Boosting

Ego-boosting is another core part of most hypnotherapy sessions. It is designed to build on the positive suggestions made during therapy. In the case of giving up smoking it describes the advantages you now enjoy by being a non-smoker.

These can be the financial savings, the social benefits and of course the health and fitness benefits. Ego-strengthening builds up your confidence and sets you up to remain a non-smoker. It helps to energise you to look forward into the near future and see yourself reaping the rewards of being a non-smoker.

At the end of this stage you should be feeling good about yourself and excited, ready to go forward and really enjoy the rest of your life by being the person you really want to be.

That just leaves the final section; the awakening.

Awakening

Whether your session has resulted in a light, medium or deep trance, you still have to be brought back to a fully awakened state so that you can carry on your normal life. There are a number of ways to achieve this and it may depend on the type of therapy that was given. But in most cases it will be a count-up from say one to ten.

However, it's not quite as simple as that. This is also the perfect opportunity to deliver some last minute suggestions either to boost the therapy or to enhance the ego-strengthening. This is because you can be particularly susceptive to suggestions just before waking up. It may take the form of suggesting you will wake up with a good feeling of wellbeing or that you feel relaxed and motivated to make those positive changes in your life. It depends on the client and their needs. In this case it will be a final positive push to your new healthy non-smoking future.

The counting-up will also usually contain some instructions such as "at the count of 8, you will open your eyes" and "at the count of 10, you will be fully wide awake." At the end just spend a few moments feeling good about yourself and congratulating yourself about you now being a non-smoker.

"Smoking kills.

If you're killed, you've lost a very important part of your life."

...Brooke Shields

Part 7

The Therapy Script – Stop Smoking

Have a read through the script and decide whether you would like to learn the gist of it or better, record it on any device so that you can just relax and listen. It's up to you.

But before we start, let me just repeat a couple of common sense points.

This script, recording or CD can be used as little or as often as you like. You may notice big changes after just the first session or you may feel them building up over time. There is no right or wrong way; just choose what works for you.

Find a place where you can make yourself comfortable and at a time where you will not be disturbed. But don't worry, if you have to attend to something, just open your eyes and get up. You can always start again later.

<u>However, never listen to the recoded script or CD whilst driving or using any machinery. Only listen when it is safe and appropriate to do.</u>

Now, get ready to change your life…

Script

Eye Closure

Now, make yourself comfortable. Either sit back in a chair or lie down. If you need to awaken before the session finishes, you can just open your eyes and tend to whatever needs to be done. There is no danger and no side effects. You can always start the session again when the time is more suitable for you.

Now…if you wish…just let your eyes gently close…feel the slight heaviness of your eyelids and just let them close. And when they do…become aware of the release of tension and the relaxation you feel around the eyes. Just relax them and let go. That's right…just let go and enjoy the feeling of relaxation.

Now…I want you to become aware of your breathing…become aware of the in breath and the out breath. And if you wish…just gently bring the focus of your attention to the tip of your nose…and become aware of your breathing at the tip of the nose. Feel the in breath and notice that the air feels cool. And now…breathe out and notice that the air feels a little warmer…and all of this is quite natural… and notice the gentle movement of the chest with each breath.

Now…just allow the out breath to lengthen a bit more…notice that you may feel some of your muscles begin to let go and relax down. Just continue for the next few moments to enjoy the feeling of extending the out breath a little bit more.

And whilst you do that…I'm going to tell you a little bit more about how hypnotherapy can make big positive and permanent changes to your life. Hypnotherapy is all about giving you control…control over that part of your life in which you wish to make those changes.

And we achieve this in gentle easy stages. The first is to give you control over your breathing and already you may be feeling a little more relaxed as your breathing becomes more measured…more calm…more peaceful.

And, as your breathing becomes steadier…you may notice that your muscles will begin to relax…and as they do…so your mind…your mind will become calmer…quieter…allowing the therapy to take place.

And all of this will happen without you having to try at all…in fact, all you have to do…is listen to the sound of my voice as we continue…

Progressive Relaxation

Now…as you continue to gently monitor your breathing, I'd like you to…now…bring the focus of your attention down to your feet. Become aware of your feet. Perhaps become aware of the skin around your feet.

And, as you do so…also become aware…now…that a warm wave of relaxation is entering your feet…through the toes…around the instep and heel…and up as far as the ankles.

And as it does…you may become aware that your feet feel a little warmer…perhaps a little lighter, as though filled with warm air. But whatever the sensations…your feet are beginning to feel more relaxed. So that soon…both of your feet are feeling warm, light and relaxed. Warm, light and relaxed.

Now…feel that warm wave of relaxation beginning to move up the lower legs…feel your calf muscles becoming warm and soft…warm and soft. Feel that warm wave of relaxation moving up as far as the knees. And, as it does so…feel the lower legs becoming warmer…lighter, as though filled with warm air…and beginning to feel very, very relaxed. So that soon…both of the lower legs are feeling warm, light and relaxed. Feeling safe and secure. Warm, light and relaxed.

Now…feel that warm wave of relaxation move up the rest of your legs…and as it does so, feel the rest of your legs becoming warmer…lighter, as though filled with warm air…and feeling very, very relaxed. So that soon…both of your legs are feeling warm, light and relaxed. Both of your legs are now feeling warm, light and relaxed.

Now…feel that warm wave of relaxation move up into your stomach area…and as it does so…feel the whole of your stomach area begin to feel warm…and calm. Warm and…calm. Feeling safe and secure. The whole of your stomach area is now feeling warm and calm.

And feel now that that warm wave of relaxation is moving up around the chest area…and as it does so…you feel your breathing becomes steadier and more peaceful…allowing you to go deeper and deeper relaxed.

Now…become aware that the warm wave of relaxation is now in your lower back. Feel the muscles in your lower back becoming warm and soft. Warm and soft. And feel now…that that warm wave of relaxation is beginning to move up the back…up your spine…vertebrae by vertebrae…And as it does so…you may feel your back just gently beginning to sink down…deeper and deeper…And as it does so…so you can allow yourself to go deeper and deeper asleep. Deeper and deeper asleep.

Feeling safe and secure…going deeper and deeper asleep.

Now…feel that warm wave of relaxation beginning to move across the shoulders and across the shoulder blades. And, as it does so…feel the shoulders relax and sag a little as they release any tension that might be there in the shoulders or neck.

And now feel that warm wave of relaxation begin to move down the arms…down the upper arms as far as the elbows. And as it does so…feel the upper arms become a little warmer…perhaps a little lighter…as though filled with warm air. But feel them both becoming more and more relaxed.

Both of the upper arms are now feeling warm…light and relaxed. Warm, light and relaxed.

And now…feel that warm wave of relaxation move through the elbows and down the forearms as far as the wrists. Feel the forearms becoming a little warmer, perhaps a little lighter…as though filled with that warm air. Feel both of the forearms becoming more and more relaxed. Both of the forearms are now feeling warm, light and relaxed.

Now…become aware of that warm wave of relaxation beginning to move through your wrists and into the hands and fingers. And…you can if you wish…just imagine being able to breathe out through the palms of your hands. Just imagine…you can breathe out through the palms of your hands.

And…as you do so…you may even notice that the palms of the hands feel a little warmer. With each out breathe…the palms of your hands may feel warmer.

Now…I want you to imagine…that you can just breathe out any tension…any worry…or any anxiety…through the palms of your hands. Any tension…any worry…or any anxiety…just imagine breathing them out and away…through the palms of the hands.

No matter where you feel them in your mind or body…just breathe them away…breathe them out through the palms of your hands…and let them go. And…as you do so…you can go deeper and deeper relaxed. Feeling safe and secure…deeper and deeper relaxed.

Now…become aware…that that warm wave of relaxation moves into the jaw and around the mouth. And…as it does so…feel the jaw just sag a little…releasing any tension that may be around the jaw and mouth.

And feel now…that that warm wave of relaxation…now moves up around the nose and up around the eyes. And as it reaches the eyes…you may feel that the eyes just want to gently sink back into their sockets a bit more. And…as your eyes sink gently back into their sockets…so you can allow yourself to go deeper and deeper asleep. As your eyes sink back deeper and deeper into their sockets…so you can go deeper and deeper asleep. Deeper and deeper.

And now…feel that warm wave of relaxation in the back of the neck. Feel the muscles in the back of the neck become warm and soft. Warm and soft. And as that warm wave of relaxation begins to move up the back of the head…you may feel your head just wants to gently sink back…deeper and deeper…as that warm wave of relaxation moves up to the top of the head.

So that soon…from the top of your head to the bottom of your feet…you are feeling warm…light…and relaxed. From the top of your head to the bottom of your feet…you are feeling warm, light…and very, very relaxed.

Now…become aware that that warm wave of relaxation begins to move down…down into your mind. And as it does so…your mind becomes calm…your mind becomes calm. Any ripples become a flat calm. Your mind becomes calm and peaceful.

And…you can now…if you wish…allow your mind to drift to a place where you feel completely relaxed…a place where you feel completely safe and secure…a special place of relaxation for you. It can be anywhere of your choosing…a past holiday…your own home…anywhere where you can just totally let go. And you can spend as much time as you wish there…and just enjoy the feelings of happiness and peace…as we go on.

Deepening

In a few seconds time you will hear me countdown from ten to one. And with each descending number between ten and one, you are going to become one tenth more relaxed.

Ten per cent more relaxed with each descending number. Each descending number will help you go one tenth deeper into that wonderful hypnotic state of relaxation; the light trance state that in any event, will become deeper and deeper as we go on.

If while I am counting, you would experience a slight, though very pleasant physical sensation; as if you were floating, floating down; that will be fine. It only means that you are drifting into an ever deepening state of physical as well as mental state of relaxation. And it will become deeper and deeper as we go on.

So ready, ten, nine. Deeper and deeper. Eight, Seven Six. Drifting down, ever deeper relaxed. Five, four, three. Deeper and deeper still. Two, One. All the way deep down relaxed.

Now…as you relax there…I want you to know that there is a very special and unique part of you…your unconscious mind…and your unconscious mind has all of the strengths and inner resources to bring about new positive changes in your life. It is the most powerful part of your mind.

And your unconscious mind can make all of these new positive changes happen without you having to try at all. It all happens naturally and without any effort on your part.

In a few moments time, you will hear me say the word...NOWwww a whenever you hear me say the word...NOWwww, every muscle in your body...from the top of your head...to the tips of your toes is relaxing. All the unnecessary nervous tension will be going out of your body and your body will continue to sink down...more and more limp, relaxed and comfortable too.

In fact your body is going to feel so pleasantly comfortable, there may be times when you will not even be aware of your body...won't be aware at all. So, if you have any unnecessary nervous tension...in any part of your body, I want you to...NOWwww...let go of that unnecessary nervous tension.

Allow every muscle in your body to relax. And soon, a very pleasant, slightly warm sensation may very soon begin to spread from your chest and shoulders and out over your whole body.

And I want you to...NOWwww...let this wonderful feeling of relaxation go all the way down, down through your body...right down to your fingertips. Your whole body feels so relaxed and comfortable.

And NOWww...as you continue to drift, I want you to know that one of the nicest things about hypnosis, is that in the trance state, you can do anything you want, just like in a pleasant dream. You can go anywhere you like...drift away...to any place...to any situation you desire...and you can enjoy any pleasant sensations you wish. They all belong to you. You can even go back in time.

Back in time to a pleasant memory. Drift back to something pleasant you haven't thought of in a long...long while. And once there, you can once again...enjoy that experience with all the feelings you had back then.

So now...I want to talk to your subconscious mind about a matter of importance...a matter of importance to you...

Therapy

You are about to say no to cigarettes for the rest of your life. No more will you feel constrained and controlled by them. You are about to break free of the burden of smoking.

And because it is your decision to stop smoking...your decision alone...then your subconscious mind will help bring all this about without any undue effort.

You have made the decision to stop smoking...and from now on...you are a non-smoker...you are a non-smoker...and that means...you never smoke...you never smoke again.

Remember back to that first cigarette you ever had...perhaps you had it because your friends smoked...and you felt pressurised into joining in. But you didn't like it...your body didn't like it...didn't like it at all. It didn't taste nice...perhaps it even made you feel sick.

But you persisted...and eventually...your body had to accept the fact that you smoked. But it didn't like it...and it still doesn't. Your body hates the fact that you smoke.

And...when in the past...you may have tried to give up...your body didn't understand that you were trying to give up. It didn't understand at all that you were trying to give up...and couldn't help you.

But now…your unconscious mind does understand…it knows what you really want…what you really desire. It knows that you are about to become and remain…a non-smoker…a non-smoker.

And your unconscious mind can communicate the fact…that you are a non-smoker…to every part of your body. So that from now on…your body will know…and be happy… that you are a non-smoker.

Now…I want you to mentally tell each part of your body…that you are a non-smoker now.

Tell your hands you are a non-smoker now.

Tell your feet and legs that you are a non-smoker now.

Tell your arms you are a non-smoker now.

Tell your stomach that you are a non-smoker now.

Tell your heart you are a non-smoker now.

And tell your lungs you are a non-smoker now.

Tell your lips and mouth you are a non-smoker now.

Tell your eyes you are a non-smoker now.

And finally…tell your mind…and agree with it now…that you are a non-smoker…agree with your mind now…that you are a non-smoker.

Make an affirmation to yourself now…I am a non-smoker…I am a non-smoker.

Remember…your whole body knows how to enjoy life without smoking…it always did…and it always will.

So therefore…you will not experience any withdrawal symptoms at all…you will not experience any withdrawal symptoms at all. In fact…your body will be happy…that for you…smoking is in the past.

And I want you to know…that you will not be substituting anything else for the cigarettes…you have left in the past. You will not eat anything more than your normal, healthy eating patterns. You will not snack…or substitute any food for the cigarettes you have left in the past.

If at any time…you feel you wish to do something with your hands or mouth…then have a few sips of cool, clear water…or some other non-alcoholic drink. And you will find…that your mind and body…will be fully satisfied…will be fully satisfied by a few sips of cool, clear water.

In fact…you may notice that your willpower becomes stronger…more enhanced…allowing you to make even more healthy positive decisions in your life.

Now…I want you to make the following affirmations to yourself…and make them an important…and integral part of your life.

Ready…

When you get up in the morning…you have no desire to smoke.

At breakfast…you have no desire to smoke.

Going to work…you have no desire to smoke.

At work…and it doesn't matter what you do…you have no desire to smoke.

At lunchtime…you have no desire to smoke.

In the afternoon…you have no desire to smoke.

Going home in the evening…you have no desire to smoke.

Before, during…and after dinner…you have no desire to smoke.

When you are relaxing at home…reading…listening to music…or watching the TV…you have no desire to smoke.

And finally…when you are out socialising…and it doesn't matter if it is with family…friends…colleagues…or even with strangers…you have no desire to smoke.

In fact…if you are ever offered a cigarette…or if you are asked if you smoke…you will be pleased and proud to say…I don't smoke…I don't smoke.

In the future…if you are ever offered a cigarette…or if you are asked if you smoke…you will be pleased and proud to say…I don't smoke…I don't smoke.

And the more times you say…I don't smoke…I don't smoke…your determination to remain a non-smoker…will be reinforced. Every time you say…I don't smoke…I don't smoke…your determination to remain a non-smoker will be reinforced.

Now…imagine for a moment…the worst smell and taste you can think of. Make it something you really find revolting. A food or substance you really hate the smell and taste of. It doesn't matter what you choose…only that it is something you find sickening

Thought of something? Good.

Now…imagine holding a lighted cigarette in your hand. Look at it…and slowly bring it towards your mouth. As it gets closer…you begin to smell that revolting odour that you have selected.

Hold it there for a moment…and just let that horrible smell enter your nostrils. Breathe it in for a few moments. It smells revolting…and you hate it.

Now…bring the cigarette a bit closer to your mouth…and know that if it touches your lips and tongue…it will taste of the same revolting substance you have thought of. To bring it any closer…and it would touch your tongue. You begin to feel that taste in your mouth. Anymore and you may feel sick.

So…take the cigarette away from your mouth…and throw it away. Get rid of it now. And when it's gone…take a deep breath of clean, fresh air. Feel the goodness and clean taste in your mouth… and the freshness of the air entering your lungs…making you feel energised.

You will never want to smell or taste a cigarette again.

And now…relax your mind completely.

And I want you to know now…that you are a non-smoker…and that means…you no longer smoke. In fact…you will never smoke tobacco in any form ever again. You will never smoke tobacco in any form ever again.

And because it's your choice never to smoke again…you will forget about smoking…forget about smoking…forget.

But if thoughts about smoking ever do pop into your mind…don't worry…don't try to fight the thought…just relax…and soon your mind will wander onto something else. You will remain a non-smoker.

And when you see other people smoking…and it's a fact of life that some people still smoke…it will mean nothing to you…it will mean nothing to you at all. You are a non-smoker…and are proud…and delighted to be a non-smoker.

And just take a moment…to realise all the new advantages you are going to have as a non-smoker. Your health will receive a boost…and you will start to feel fitter and healthier as the weeks go by. Your senses of smell and taste will come back…and you will be able to enjoy the smell of fresh air.

Imagine taking a deep breath…and allowing all of that fresh air into your lungs…letting it energise you…ready to enjoy life more than you have for a long time.

But besides the health benefits…think of the financial benefits…the money that you are now saving. In the past…buying 10 cigarettes a day would cost you a total of nearly £900 in a year.

And I want you to save that money…to put it aside. And I want you to use it to treat yourself. To use it on something to give you pleasure. It may be a holiday…membership of a gym…or even a new wardrobe of clothes. It's up to you…but it is your reward to yourself…for giving up cigarettes…leaving them behind you in the past…and becoming a non-smoker.

And finally…I'm going to ask you a question…and you must answer it yes or no…and you must answer it honestly to yourself.

This is your final affirmation to yourself...the seal on the start of your new healthy life.

Ready? Answer yes or no.

Are you a non-smoker now?

And if your answer is yes...then you are a non-smoker now.

The part of you that used to smoke is now gone...and you can move forward into your new positive and healthy life...feeling free to really enjoy your life by being the person you really are.

Ego-Boosting

Now…because you are feeling so very relaxed…your mind has become so sensitive…so receptive to what I say…that everything I have said has sunk deeply into your unconscious mind…and will cause such a lasting impression there…that nothing will be able to eradicate it.

Consequently…these positive suggestions I have made to your subconscious mind are now a part of the real you. And over the days…weeks and months…these positive suggestions will grow stronger and stronger within you.

And still more positive changes will begin to happen to you…as I now make new suggestions to your unconscious mind.

You let go of the old fears and anxieties…and in their place…you have new powerful coping skills…new tools that will give you…control over your fears…control over your stresses…and control over any negative thoughts and habits that you used to have.

Each day…you grow stronger…more confident…more self-assured…you will now find you can cope with any situation that arises. And you will be able to cope also with any negative feelings…no matter how they arise.

And that is because…you have learned…how to relax…and feel more confident in your own abilities. The old fears and habits are now in the past…they are far behind you…and you will find that with each passing day…they will fade even more.

And in their place…is your new healthier blueprint for the future…a future where you feel happier and more confident in your own abilities.

So…look ahead and imagine for a moment the new you standing in front of you. See how the new you stands…see how the new you looks…talks…and acts with others. And see how confident you look in your own new body.

Now…I want you to step inside the new you. Just take a step forward and become one with the new you. That's right…and when you have done so…look through their eyes…hear through their ears…feel what they feel…and now…feel how good it is to be the new you.

Feel comfortable in your new body…and begin to enjoy your new abilities…the calmness…the quiet self-confidence…the joy of being the new you. Really get to know and like the new you.

And don't worry about having to leave the new you…because the new you…is you…and it is here to stay.

And when I awaken you...you will wake up as the new...real you...with a feeling of confidence and wellbeing...ready to enjoy life...by being the person you really are.

Awakening

Now…in a few moments…I'm going to awaken you. You'll hear me count from 1 to 10…and with each ascending number from 1 to 10…you will come slowly awake. At the count of 8…you will open your eyes…and at the count of 10…you will be fully wide awake. You will wake up feeling fine…with a feeling of wellbeing all over.

Every part of you will be back here with me in the present…except those negative parts that have been left in the past. But all the normal sensations will return to your body.

So you'll hear me count from 1 to 10. And with each ascending number…you will come slowly more awake. At the count of 8…you will open your eyes…and at the count of 10…you will be wide awake.

So ready…1, 2, 3…waking up slowly…4, 5, 6…waking up more quickly now…7, 8…open your eyes…open your eyes…9, 10…fully wide awake…fully wide awake. And ready to really enjoy your life.

Post Trance

When you open your eyes, you should be feeling very relaxed as you should after every trance session. However, your state of relaxation may be such that you may feel a little light-headed or a little disorientated.

Don't worry, this is quite normal. So just spend a couple of minutes relaxing and fully coming awake. It can be very much like coming out of a deep and relaxing sleep. Don't rush it, just enjoy the feel-good sensations.

"The cigarette does the smoking-

You're just the sucker."

…Author Unknown

Part 8

The Way Ahead

Hypnotherapy can work in different ways for different people. Using a registered hypnotherapist can often result in never touching cigarettes ever again after just one session. For others the change may be more gradual. Using this guide can bring about positive changes.

For some, just reading the book and the therapy script will be enough to stop them smoking forever. If you are really ready to quit, it can happen as easy as that. If it doesn't happen for you straight away, do not give up (you only need to give up the cigarettes). Use the script in different ways as outlined earlier.

You may find that if your trigger to smoke has been stress, then just practicing the progressive relaxation may be sufficient to take away the stimulus to smoke. What is important is that you use this guide to start to change your life. It should help you towards leaving cigarettes in the past but it will also help you to relax and see things in a new light; with perspective and a new understanding.

You may begin to feel more in control of your life on a day to day basis and these feelings will also help you to achieve your final goal of giving up smoking and leading a more positive and healthier lifestyle.

The consequences of not giving up can be grave but the rewards of a smoke-free future are huge and deserve your best intentions.

I wish you the best of luck but remember, in the words of the golf professional Gary Player, "The more I practice, the luckier I get."

Some Final Thoughts

"I'm more proud of quitting smoking than of anything else I've done in my life, including winning an Oscar."

...Christine Lahti

"I don't smoke and I don't want to smoke. I am not a fan of gratuitous smoking in films."

...Edward Norton

"The true face of smoking is disease, death and horror –

not the glamour and sophistication the pushers in the

tobacco industry tries to portray."

...David Byrne

"Exercise can't counteract the damage being done

to your body while you continue to smoke.

What exercise can do is help you kick the habit."

...Kenneth H. Cooper, MD

"Cigarette smoking is clearly identified as the chief, preventable cause of death in our society."

...C. Everett Koop, former Surgeon General

"Seven out of 10 people don't smoke and of those who do, seven out of 10 want to give up."

...Scottish Health Minister Andy Kerr

And finally...

"You're always better off if you quit smoking; it's never too late."

...Loni Anderson

Further Information

For further information about the author, go to

www.johnpullenwriter.com

For further information and resources about hypnotherapy, go to;-

www.hypnohealthservices.com

For information about training to become a hypnotherapist, go to;-

www.lcch.co.uk

For information in finding a registered hypnotherapist, go to;-

www.bsch.org.uk

Other Books by the same Author

<u>Non-Fiction</u>

<u>Aviation Series</u>

How to Fly a Plane

The Private Pilot Flying Course Part 1

The Private Pilot Flying Course Part 2

The Private Pilot Skill Test

The Flight Pilot Radio Manual

The Flight Pilot Instrument Rating Flying Course Part 1

The Flight Pilot Instrument Rating Flying Course Part 2

<u>Medical Series</u>

Hypnotherapy

Being Happy

Stop Smoking

www.ingramcontent.com/pod-product-compliance
Lightning Source LLC
Chambersburg PA
CBHW070427290526
45791CB00005B/1863